Spring

disc

by Tanya Thayer

first step nonfiction

It is spring.

It is getting warmer.

The days are getting longer.

Buds grow.

Birds come back.

Rain falls.

The sun comes out.

Children plant seeds.

Flowers **bloom.**

Bees buzz.

Birds build **nests.**

Baby birds **hatch.**

Cows are born.

Sheep play.

The **wind** blows.

Summer is coming.

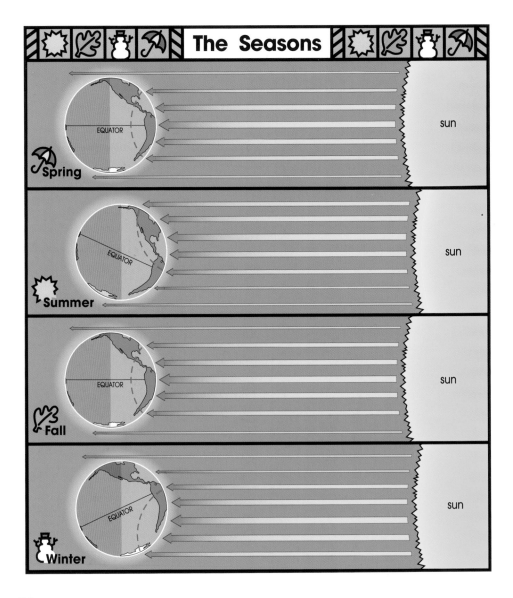

EQUATOR

Spring

EQUATOR

Summer

EQUATOR

Fall

EQUATOR

Winter

sun

sun

sun

sun

Seasons

The earth moves around the sun. The sun shines on the earth. When the sun shines mostly on the middle of the earth, it is spring in the United States.

There is more sunlight in the spring than there is in the winter. The days are longer in the spring, too. When there is more sunlight in a day, it is warmer.

Spring Facts

When birds fly from cold parts of the world to warmer parts of the world it is called migration. Warmer parts of the world have more food than colder parts. Birds migrate in the spring.

Some animals are born or hatch in the spring. It is easier for animal parents to find food for their babies in the spring.

Spring rains help seeds and new plants to grow.

When a bee lands on a flower yellow stuff called pollen sticks to the bee. When the bee lands on a new flower the pollen rubs off. Then, the flower is ready to make seeds and fruit.

If a bud gets too cold in the spring it will freeze. A bud that has frozen cannot make leaves or flowers anymore.

Glossary

 buds – the part of a plant that may make a flower

 bloom – when a flower opens

 hatch – when a baby animal comes out of its' egg

 nests – a place where baby animals are kept safe

 wind – a natural movement of air

Index

baby animals – 13, 14, 15

birds – 6, 7, 12, 13

buds – 5

clothes – 3

flowers – 10, 11

growing animals – 13, 14, 15

seeds – 9

weather – 3, 7, 8, 16

The photographs in this book are reproduced through the courtesy of: Independent Picture Service, front cover, pp. 10, 22 (second from top); © Eugene Schulz, pp. 2, 6; © Dennis Degnan/Corbis, p. 3; © Stuart Westmoreland/CORBIS, p. 4; © Eric and David Hosking/Corbis, pp. 5, 22 (top); © Kjell B. Sandued/Visuals Unlimited, p. 7; © Stephen Graham Photography, p. 8; © Lynda Richardson/Corbis, p. 9; © Gerald and Buff Corsi/Focus on Nature, Inc., p. 11; © Richard Jacobs/Root Resources, pp. 12, 22 (second from bottom); © E. McLaury, pp. 13, 22 (middle); © Corbis, p. 14; U.S. Department of Agriculture, p. 15; © Faith Bowlus/Photo Network, pp. 16, 22 (bottom); © Stockbyte, p. 17.

This book is available in two editions:
Library binding by Lerner Publications Company, a division of Lerner Publishing Group
Soft cover by First Avenue Editions, an imprint of Lerner Publishing Group
241 First Avenue North
Minneapolis, MN 55401 USA

Website address: www.lernerbooks.com

Library of Congress Cataloging-in-Publication Data

Thayer, Tanya.
    Spring / by Tanya Thayer.
        p.   cm. — (First step nonfiction)
    Includes index.
    ISBN-13: 978-0-8225-1986-7 (lib. bdg. : alk. paper)
    ISBN-10: 0-8225-1986-0 (lib. bdg. : alk. paper)
    ISBN-13: 978-0-8225-1990-4 (pbk. : alk. paper)
    ISBN-10: 0-8225-1990-9 (pbk. : alk. paper)
    1. Spring—Juvenile literature. [1. Spring.] I. Title. II. Series.
QB637.5.T44 2002
508.2—dc21   2001000536

Manufactured in the United States of America
6 7 8 9 10 11 – DP – 11 10 09 08 07 06